Add Using Number Line

Problem 1:

$$5 + 1 =$$

Using the Number line to addition

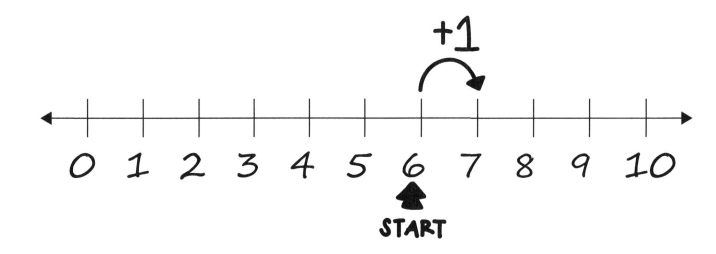

Add Using Number Line

Problem 2:

$$3 + 2 =$$

Using the Number line to addition

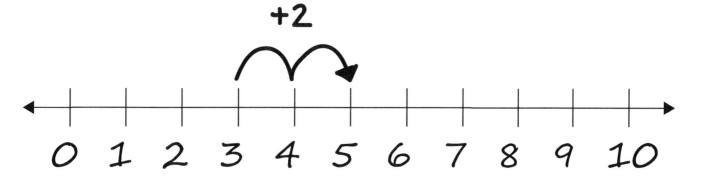

Add Using Number Line

Problem 3:

$$4 + 5 =$$

Using the Number line to addition

+5

0 1 2 3 4 5 6 7 8 9 10

Add Using Number Line

Problem 4:

$$7 + 3 =$$

Using the Number line to addition

Add Using Number Line

Problem 5:

$$5 + 2 =$$

Using the Number line to addition

+2

0 1 2 3 4 5 6 7 8 9 10

Add Using Number Line

Problem 6:

$$6 + 3 =$$

Using the Number line to addition

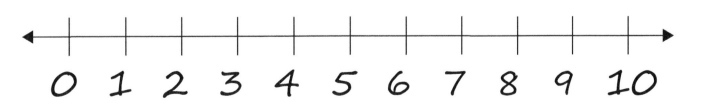

Add Using Number Line

Problem 7:

$$3 + 5 =$$

Using the Number line to addition

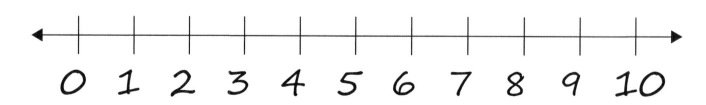

0 1 2 3 4 5 6 7 8 9 10

Add Using Number Line

Problem 8:

$$2 + 6 =$$

Using the Number line to addition

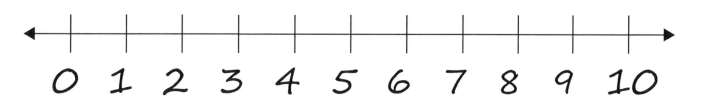

Add Using Number Line

Problem 9:

$$1 + 7 =$$

Using the Number line to addition

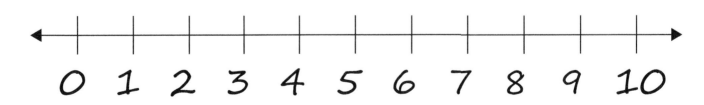

Add Using Number Line

Problem 10:

$$5 + 4 =$$

Using the Number line to addition

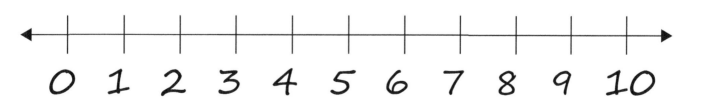

0 1 2 3 4 5 6 7 8 9 10

Add Using Number Line

Problem 11:

$$2 + 1 =$$

Using the Number line to addition

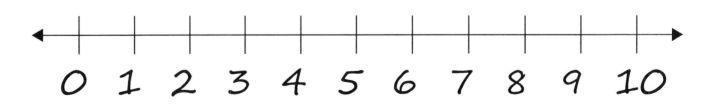

Add Using Number Line

Problem 12:

$$1 + 8 =$$

Using the Number line to addition

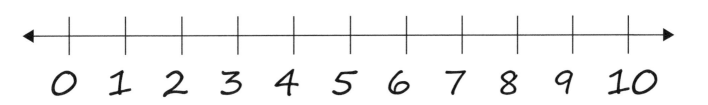

Add Using Number Line

Problem 13:

3 + 4 =

Using the Number line to addition

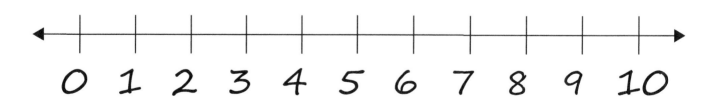

0 1 2 3 4 5 6 7 8 9 10

Add Using Number Line

Problem 14:

$$4 + 2 =$$

Using the Number line to addition

0 1 2 3 4 5 6 7 8 9 10

Add Using Number Line

Problem 15:

$$2 + 2 =$$

Using the Number line to addition

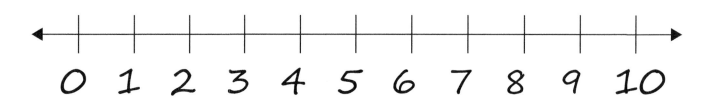

0 1 2 3 4 5 6 7 8 9 10

Add Using Number Line

Problem 16:

$$1 + 1 =$$

Using the Number line to addition

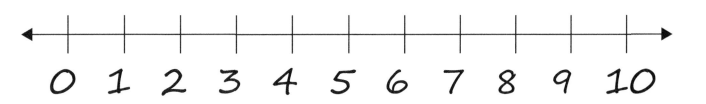

0 1 2 3 4 5 6 7 8 9 10

Add Using Number Line

Problem 17:

$$2 + 1 =$$

Using the Number line to addition

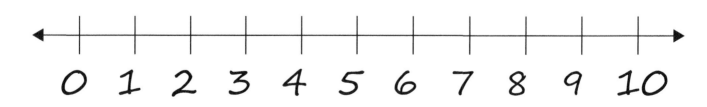

Add Using Number Line

Problem 18:

$$5 + 2 =$$

Using the Number line to addition

Add Using Number Line

Problem 19:

$$4 + 1 =$$

Using the Number line to addition

0 1 2 3 4 5 6 7 8 9 10

Add Using Number Line

Problem 20:

$$4 + 2 =$$

Using the Number line to addition

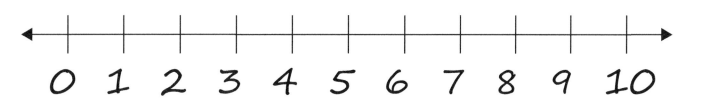

0 1 2 3 4 5 6 7 8 9 10

Add Using Number Line

Problem 21:

$$1 + 3 =$$

Using the Number line to addition

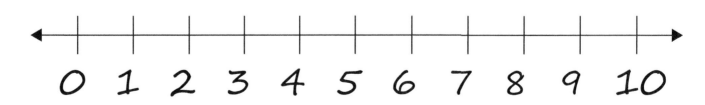

Add Using Number Line

Problem 22:

$$3 + 2 =$$

Using the Number line to addition

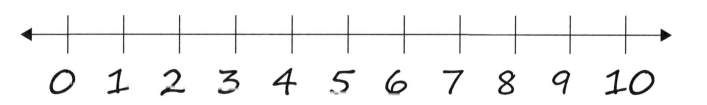

Add Using Number Line

Problem 23:

$$4 + 6 =$$

Using the Number line to addition

Add Using Number Line

Problem 24:

$$6 + 2 =$$

Using the Number line to addition

0 1 2 3 4 5 6 7 8 9 10

Add Using Number Line

Problem 25:

$$8 + 1 =$$

Using the Number line to addition

```
<---+---+---+---+---+---+---+---+---+---+---+--->
    0   1   2   3   4   5   6   7   8   9   10
```

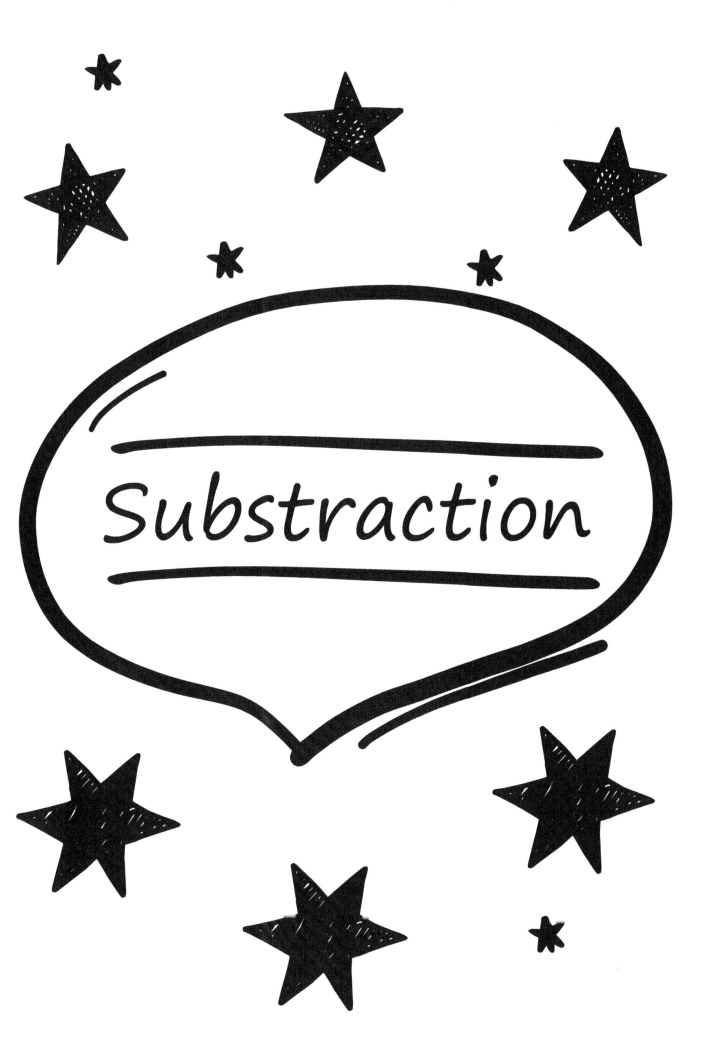

Subtract Using Number Line

Problem 26:

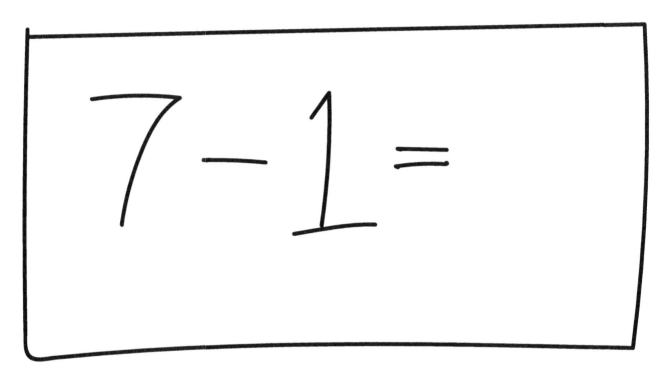

$$7 - 1 =$$

Using the Number line to subtraction

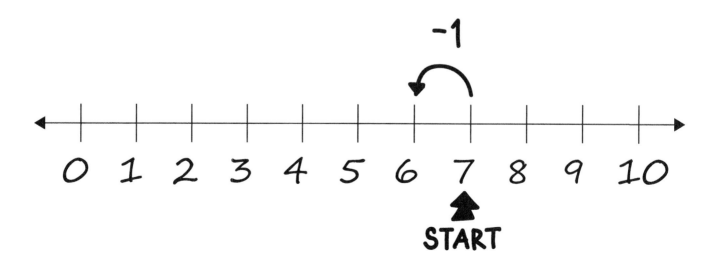

Subtract Using Number Line

Problem 27:

$$5 - 2 =$$

Using the Number line to subtraction

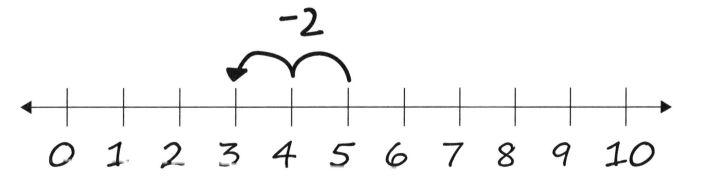

Subtract Using Number Line

Problem 28:

$$9 - 3 =$$

Using the Number line to subtraction

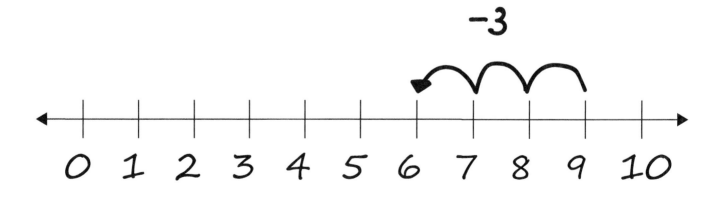

Subtract Using Number Line

Problem 29:

$$8 - 4 =$$

Using the Number line to subtraction

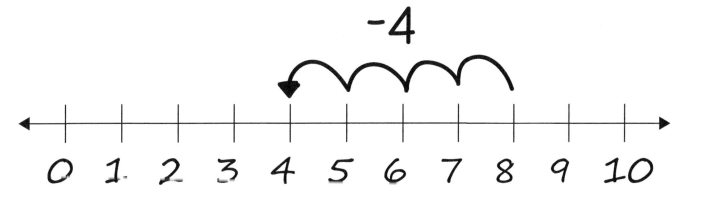

Subtract Using Number Line

Problem 30:

$$5 - 4 =$$

Using the Number line to subtraction

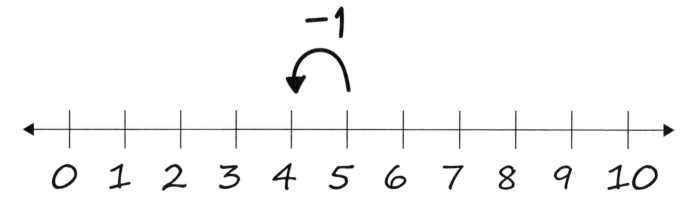

Subtract Using Number Line

Problem 31:

$$7 - 2 =$$

Using the Number line to subtraction

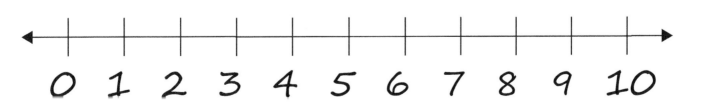

Subtract Using Number Line

Problem 32:

6 - 1 =

Using the Number line to subtraction

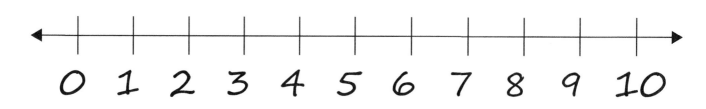

0　1　2　3　4　5　6　7　8　9　10

Subtract Using Number Line

Problem 33:

$$9 - 8 =$$

Using the Number line to subtraction

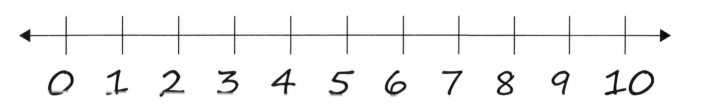

Subtract Using Number Line

Problem 34:

$$10 - 4 =$$

Using the Number line to subtraction

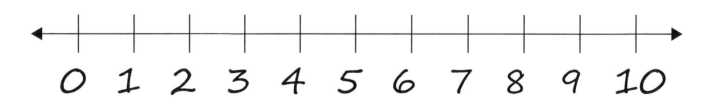

Subtract Using Number Line

Problem 35:

$$8 - 3 =$$

Using the Number line to subtraction

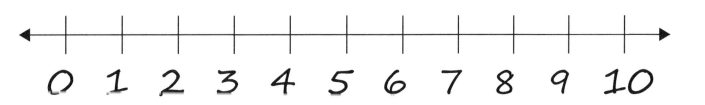

Subtract Using Number Line

Problem 36:

$$4 - 2 =$$

Using the Number line to subtraction

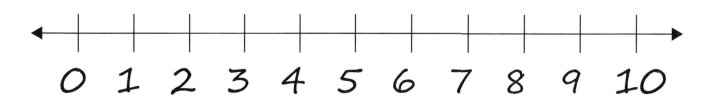

Subtract Using Number Line

Problem 37:

$$6 - 3 =$$

Using the Number line to subtraction

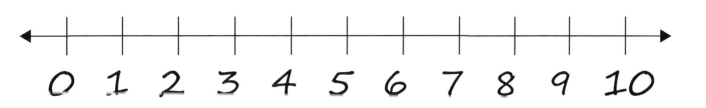

Subtract Using Number Line

Problem 38:

$$4 - 1 =$$

Using the Number line to subtraction

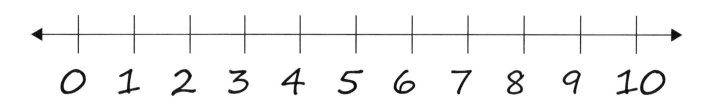

Subtract Using Number Line

Problem 39:

$$3 - 2 = $$

Using the Number line to subtraction

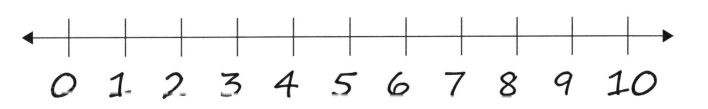

Subtract Using Number Line

Problem 40:

5 - 5 =

Using the Number line to subtraction

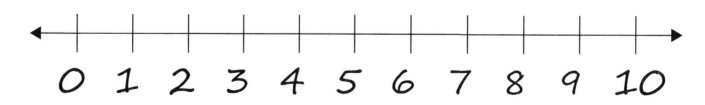

0 1 2 3 4 5 6 7 8 9 10

Subtract Using Number Line

Problem 41:

$$9 - 4 =$$

Using the Number line to subtraction

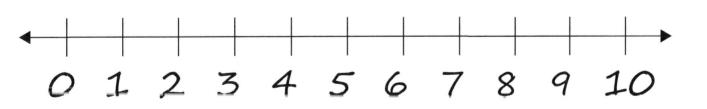

Subtract Using Number Line

Problem 42:

$$10 - 1 =$$

Using the Number line to subtraction

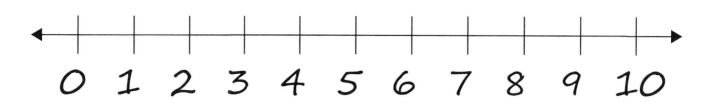

Subtract Using Number Line

Problem 43:

$$9 - 2 =$$

Using the Number line to subtraction

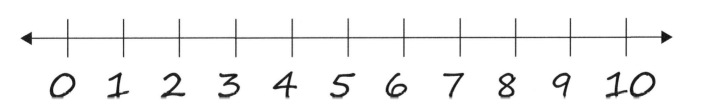

Subtract Using Number Line

Problem 44:

$$10 - 2 =$$

Using the Number line to subtraction

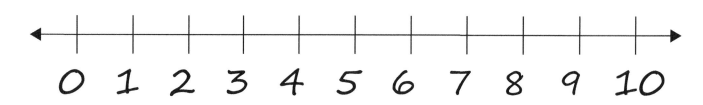

0 1 2 3 4 5 6 7 8 9 10

Subtract Using Number Line

Problem 45:

$$8 - 3 =$$

Using the Number line to subtraction

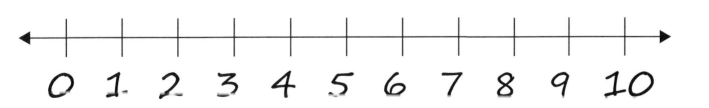

0   1   2   3   4   5   6   7   8   9   10

Subtract Using Number Line

Problem 46:

$$7 - 3 =$$

Using the Number line to subtraction

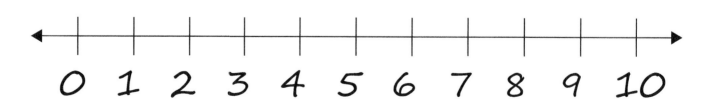

0 1 2 3 4 5 6 7 8 9 10

Subtract Using Number Line

Problem 47:

$$4 - 4 =$$

Using the Number line to subtraction

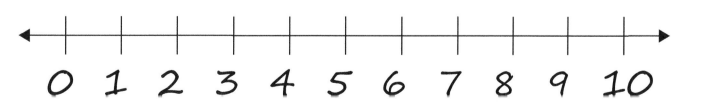

0 1 2 3 4 5 6 7 8 9 10

Subtract Using Number Line

Problem 48:

$$6 - 1 =$$

Using the Number line to subtraction

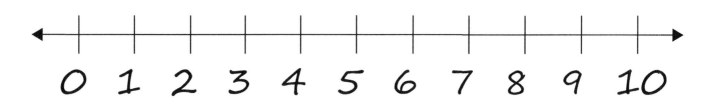

Subtract Using Number Line

Problem 49:

$$8 - 2 =$$

Using the Number line to subtraction

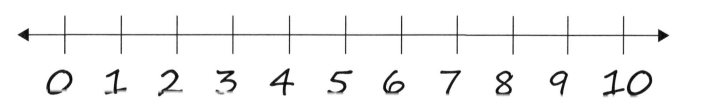

Subtract Using Number Line

Problem 50:

$$3 - 1 = $$

Using the Number line to subtraction

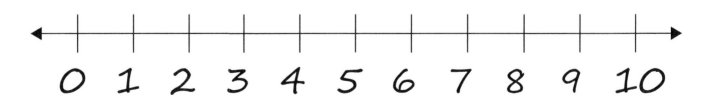

Add Using Number Line

Problem 1:

$$5 + 1 = 6$$

Using the Number line to addition

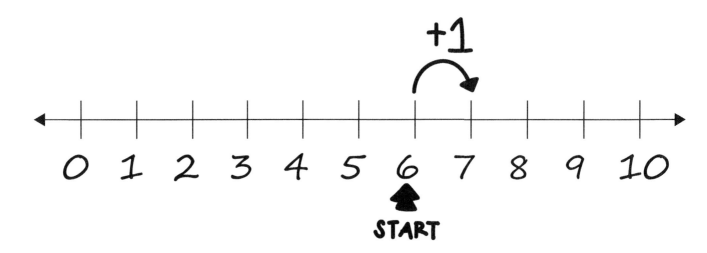

Add Using Number Line

Problem 2:

$$3 + 2 = 5$$

Using the Number line to addition

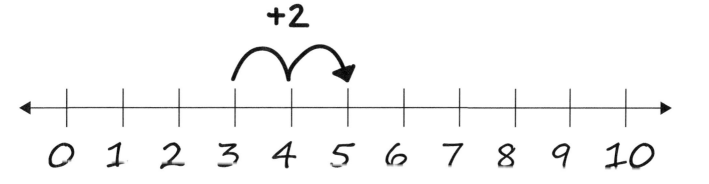

Add Using Number Line

Problem 3:

$$4 + 5 = 9$$

Using the Number line to addition

+5

0 1 2 3 4 5 6 7 8 9 10

Add Using Number Line

Problem 4:

$$7 + 3 = 10$$

Using the Number line to addition

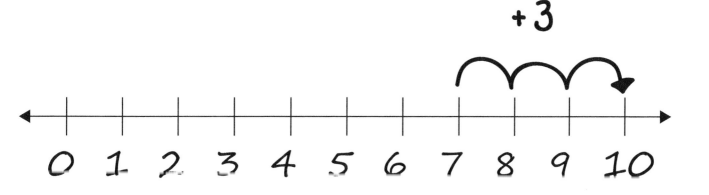

+3

Add Using Number Line

Problem 5:

$$5 + 2 = 7$$

Using the Number line to addition

+2

0 1 2 3 4 5 6 7 8 9 10

Add Using Number Line

Problem 6:

$$6 + 3 = 9$$

Using the Number line to addition

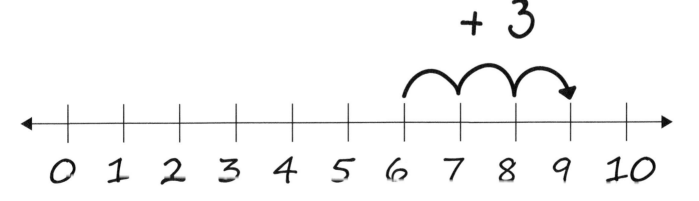

+ 3

Add Using Number Line

Problem 7:

$$3 + 5 = 8$$

Using the Number line to addition

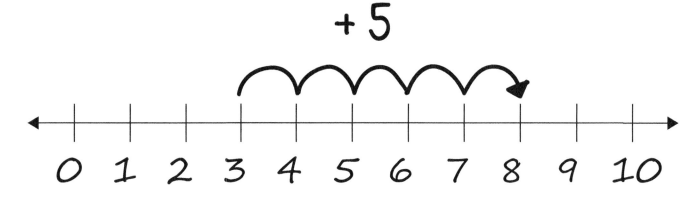

+5

Add Using Number Line

Problem 8:

$$2 + 6 = 8$$

Using the Number line to addition

+6

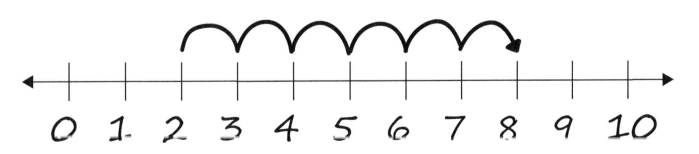

Add Using Number Line

Problem 9:

$$1 + 7 = 8$$

Using the Number line to addition

+7

0 1 2 3 4 5 6 7 8 9 10

Add Using Number Line

Problem 10:

$$5 + 4 = 9$$

Using the Number line to addition

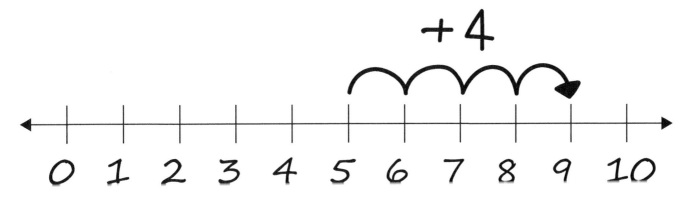

Add Using Number Line

Problem 11:

$$2 + 1 = 3$$

Using the Number line to addition

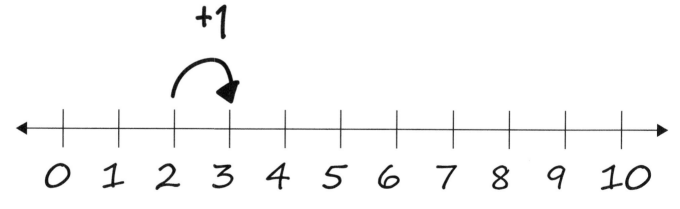

Add Using Number Line

Problem 12:

$$1 + 8 = 9$$

Using the Number line to addition

+ 8

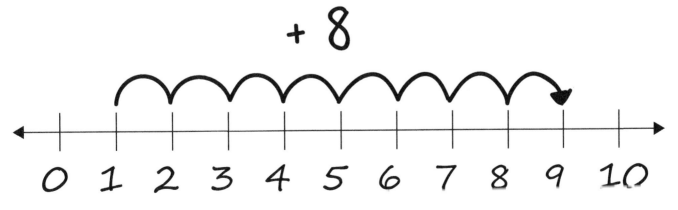

0 1 2 3 4 5 6 7 8 9 10

Add Using Number Line

Problem 13:

$$3 + 4 = 7$$

Using the Number line to addition

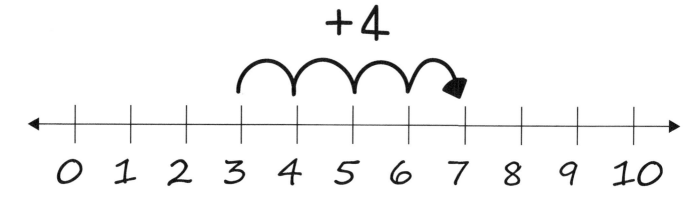

+4

0 1 2 3 4 5 6 7 8 9 10

Add Using Number Line

Problem 14:

$$3 + 3 = 6$$

Using the Number line to addition

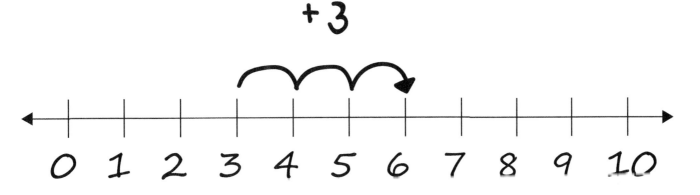

+3

0 1 2 3 4 5 6 7 8 9 10

Add Using Number Line

Problem 15:

$$2 + 2 = 4$$

Using the Number line to addition

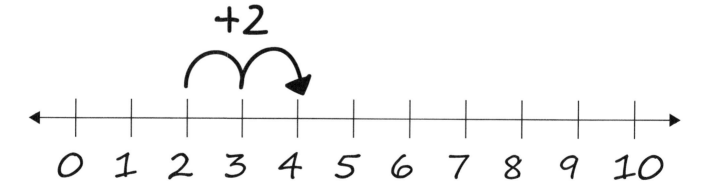

Add Using Number Line

Problem 16:

$$1 + 1 = 2$$

Using the Number line to addition

Add Using Number Line

Problem 17:

$$2 + 1 = 3$$

Using the Number line to addition

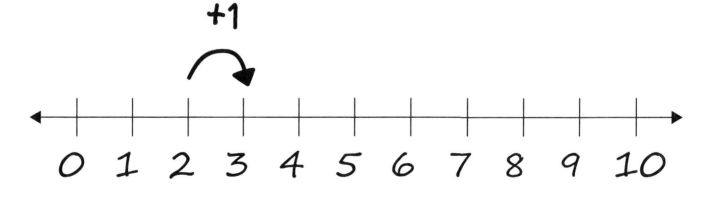

Add Using Number Line

Problem 18:

$$5 + 2 = 7$$

Using the Number line to addition

+2

0 1 2 3 4 5 6 7 8 9 10

Add Using Number Line

Problem 19:

$$4 + 1 = 5$$

Using the Number line to addition

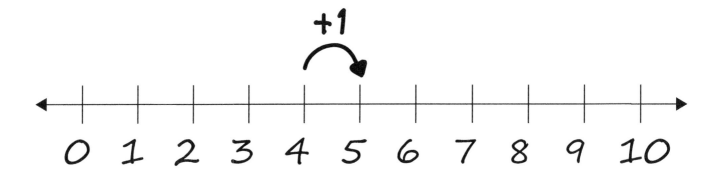

Add Using Number Line

Problem 20:

$$4 + 2 = 6$$

Using the Number line to addition

+ 2

0 1 2 3 4 5 6 7 8 9 10

Add Using Number Line

Problem 21:

$$1 + 3 = 4$$

Using the Number line to addition

+ 3

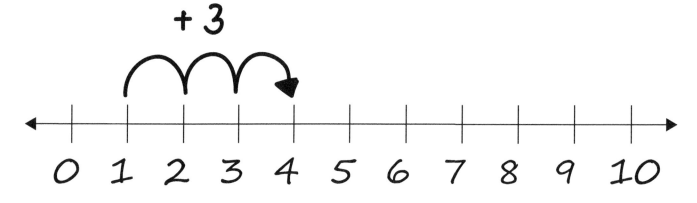

Add Using Number Line

Problem 22:

$$3 + 2 = 5$$

Using the Number line to addition

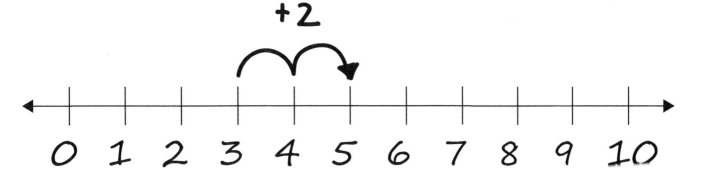

Add Using Number Line

Problem 23:

$$4 + 6 = 10$$

Using the Number line to addition

+6

0 1 2 3 4 5 6 7 8 9 10

Add Using Number Line

Problem 24:

$$6 + 2 = 8$$

Using the Number line to addition

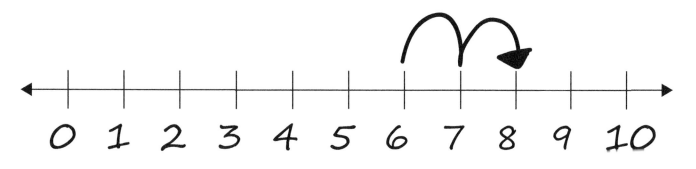

+2

0 1 2 3 4 5 6 7 8 9 10

Add Using Number Line

Problem 25:

$$8 + 1 = 9$$

Using the Number line to addition

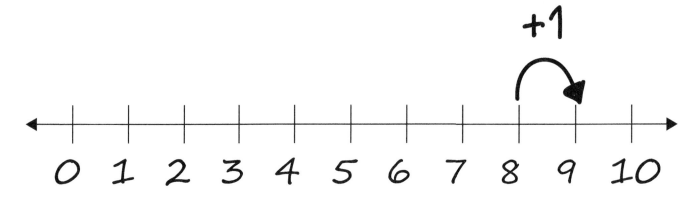

Subtract Using a Number Line

Problem 26:

$$7 - 1 = 6$$

Using the Number line to Subtraction

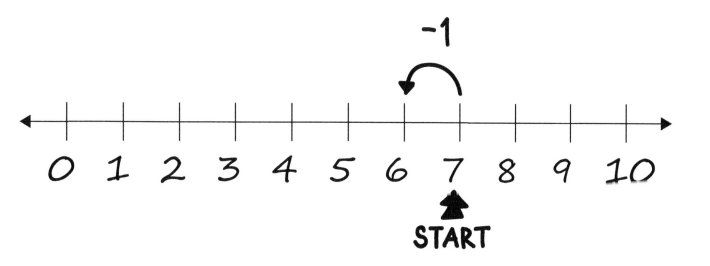

Subtract Using a Number Line

Problem 27:

$$5 - 2 = 3$$

Using the Number line to Subtraction

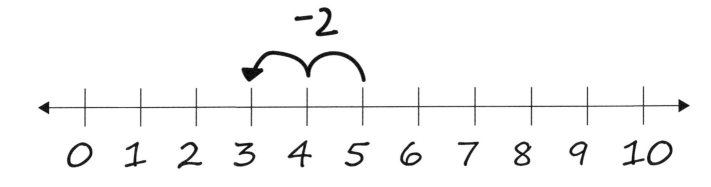

Subtract Using a Number Line

Problem 28:

$$9 - 3 = 6$$

Using the Number line to Subtraction

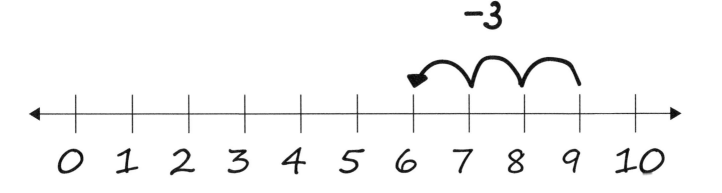

-3

Subtract Using a Number Line

Problem 29:

$$8 - 4 = 4$$

Using the Number line to Subtraction

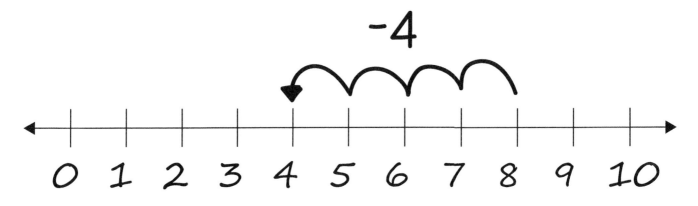

Subtract Using a Number Line

Problem 30:

$$5 - 4 = 1$$

Using the Number line to Subtraction

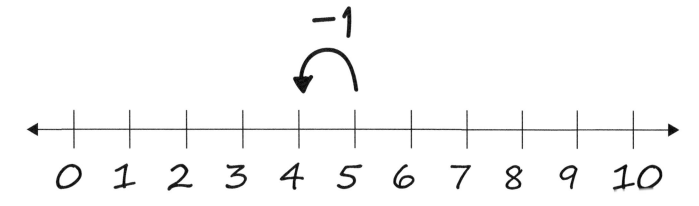

Subtract Using a Number Line

Problem 31:

$$7 - 2 = 5$$

Using the Number line to Subtraction

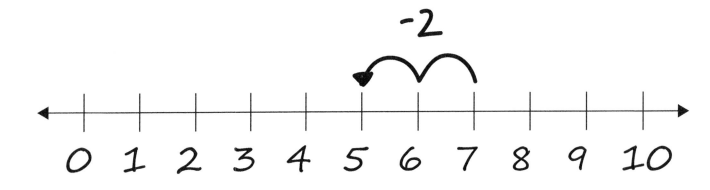

Subtract Using a Number Line

Problem 32:

$$6 - 1 = 5$$

Using the Number line to Subtraction

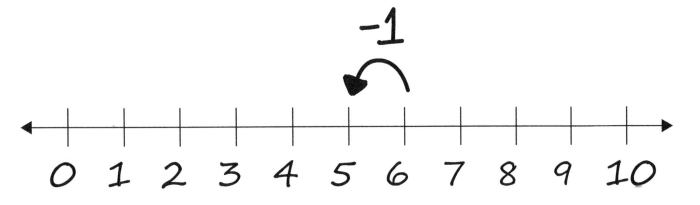

Subtract Using a Number Line

Problem 33:

$$9 - 8 = 1$$

Using the Number line to Subtraction

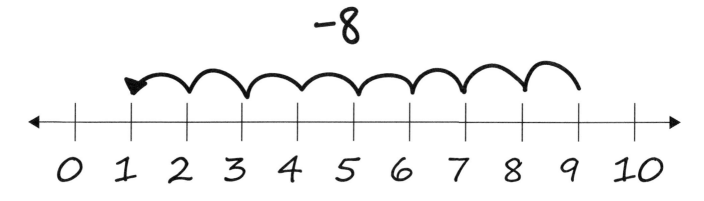

-8

0 1 2 3 4 5 6 7 8 9 10

Subtract Using a Number Line

Problem 34:

$$10 - 4 = 6$$

Using the Number line to Subtraction

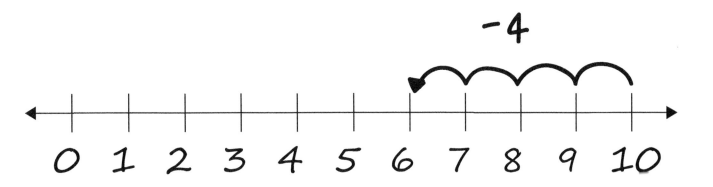

Subtract Using a Number Line

Problem 35:

$$8 - 3 = 5$$

Using the Number line to Subtraction

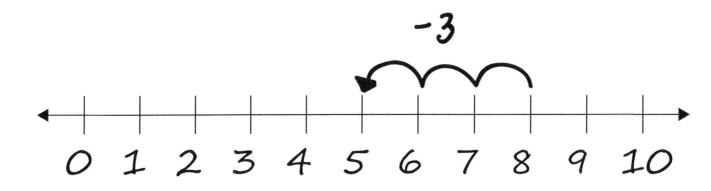

Subtract Using a Number Line

Problem 36:

$$4 - 2 = 2$$

Using the Number line to Subtraction

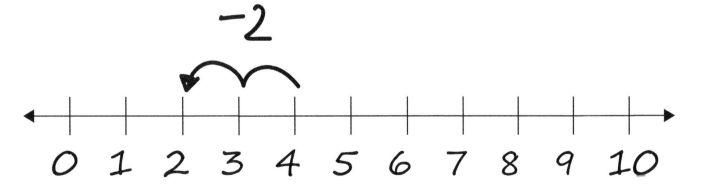

Subtract Using a Number Line

Problem 37:

$$6 - 3 = 3$$

Using the Number line to Subtraction

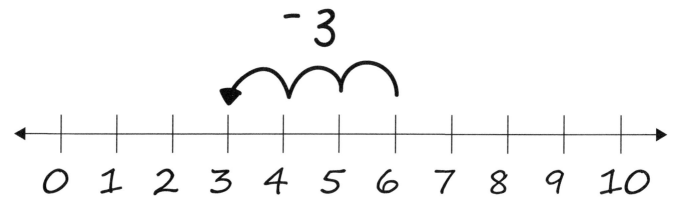

Subtract Using a Number Line

Problem 38:

$$4 - 1 = 3$$

Using the Number line to Subtraction

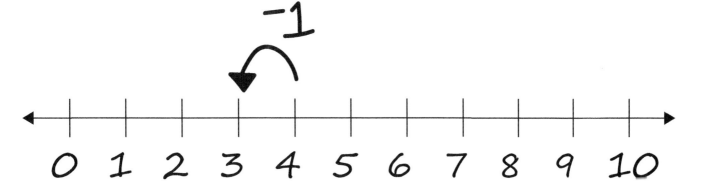

Subtract Using a Number Line

Problem 39:

$$3 - 2 = 1$$

Using the Number line to Subtraction

Subtract Using a Number Line

Problem 40:

$$5 - 5 = 0$$

Using the Number line to Subtraction

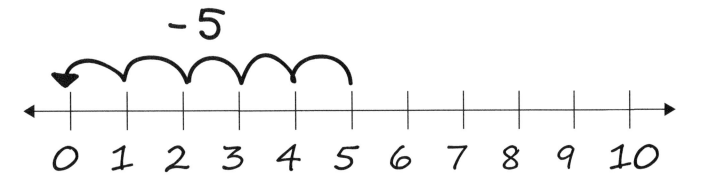

-5

0 1 2 3 4 5 6 7 8 9 10

Subtract Using a Number Line

Problem 41:

$$9 - 4 = 5$$

Using the Number line to Subtraction

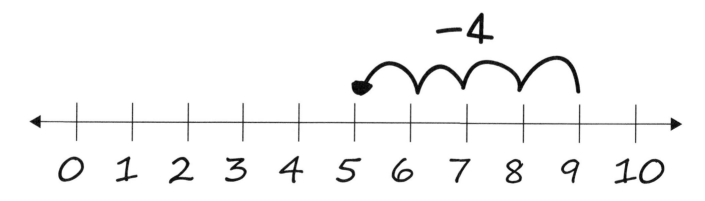

Subtract Using a Number Line

Problem 42:

$$10 - 1 = 9$$

Using the Number line to Subtraction

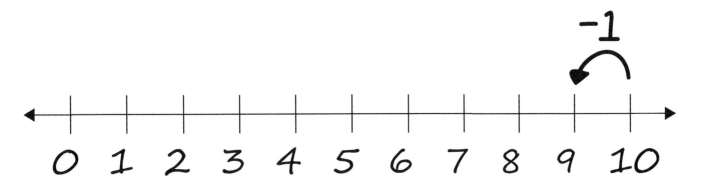

Subtract Using a Number Line

Problem 43:

$$9 - 2 = 7$$

Using the Number line to Subtraction

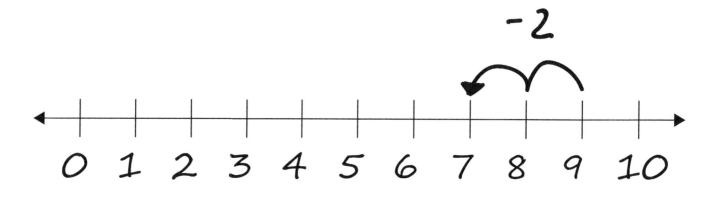

-2

0 1 2 3 4 5 6 7 8 9 10

Subtract Using a Number Line

Problem 44:

$$10 - 2 = 8$$

Using the Number line to Subtraction

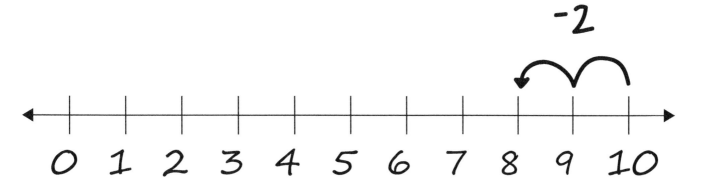

Subtract Using a Number Line

Problem 45:

$$8 - 3 = 5$$

Using the Number line to Subtraction

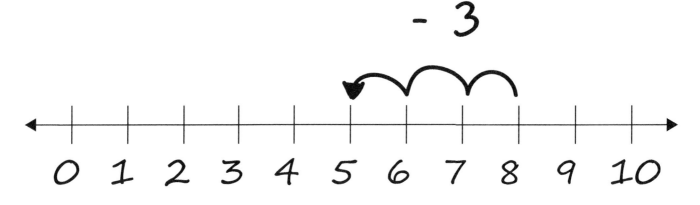

- 3

0 1 2 3 4 5 6 7 8 9 10

Subtract Using a Number Line

Problem 46:

$$7 - 3 = 4$$

Using the Number line to Subtraction

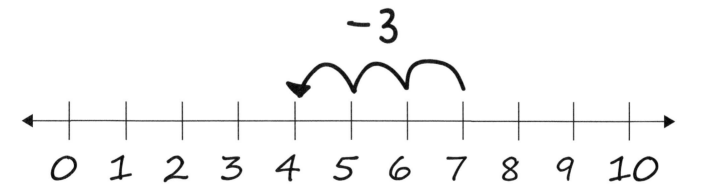

Subtract Using a Number Line

Problem 47:

$$4 - 4 = 0$$

Using the Number line to Subtraction

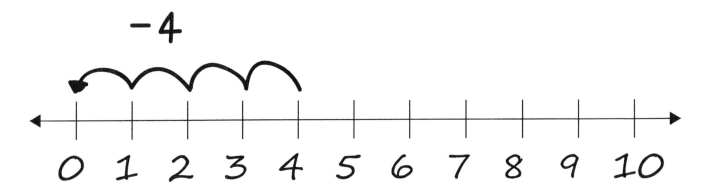

−4

0 1 2 3 4 5 6 7 8 9 10

Subtract Using a Number Line

Problem 48:

$$6 - 1 = 5$$

Using the Number line to Subtraction

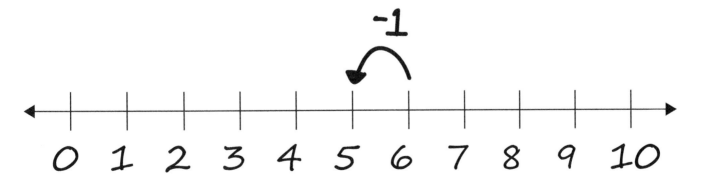

Subtract Using a Number Line

Problem 49:

$$8 - 2 = 6$$

Using the Number line to Subtraction

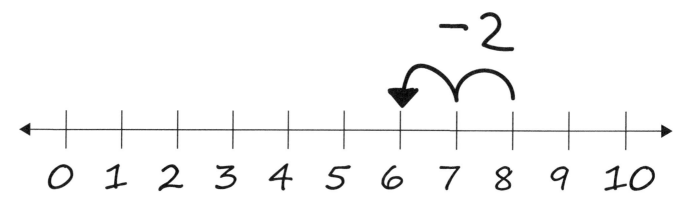

-2

0 1 2 3 4 5 6 7 8 9 10

Subtract Using a Number Line

Problem 50:

$$3 - 1 = 2$$

Using the Number line to Subtraction

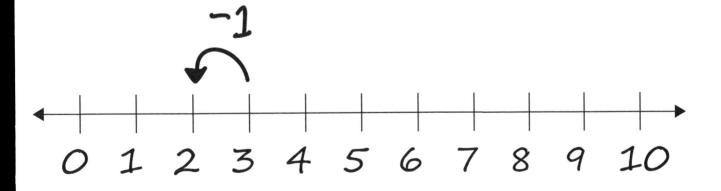

Printed in Great Britain
by Amazon